CONTENTS

THE FORMATION OF THE EARTH

WHEN DID THE EARTH FORM?

Earth began to form about **4,600 million years ago.** Scholars have divided the history of its formation into **five geological eras.** These eras have left traces which allow us to study and understand the changes our planet has undergone.

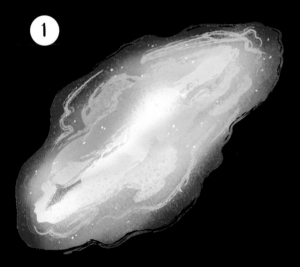

HOW DID EARTH FORM?

Initially Earth was a **cloud of gas and dust**. There were many other clouds, which all together formed our Solar System.

The **Sun** was one of these clouds: it began to rotate, becoming hotter and condensing.

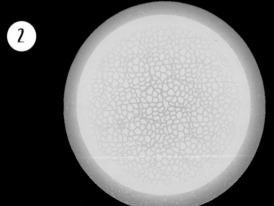

Then the **planets** formed: smaller collections of matter which were not as hot as the Sun.

This is how **Earth** was born, which very slowly took its spherical shape, a little flattened at each pole.

HAS EARTH ALWAYS BEEN A HOSPITABLE PLACE?

No. For several million years, Earth was somewhat **inhospitable**. Before the presence of oxygen, it did not have an atmosphere. Its landscape was very bare and seemed to be on the slopes of a volcano, surrounded by magma and rock. The surface temperature was **800° C** (1472° F) and the air was unbreathable!

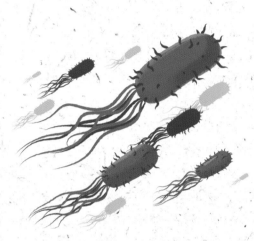

WHEN DID THE FIRST LIFE FORMS APPEAR?

About **3,500 million years ago**. They were tiny, lived only in water and were completely different from today's plant and animal species! These **microscopic life forms** are very important, because they are the starting point from which all forms of life on Earth developed.

about 225 million years ago   *about 150 million years ago*   *about 100 million years ago*   *today*

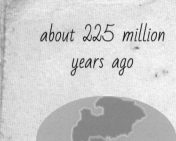
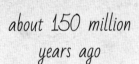

WHAT IS PANGEA?

The lands that emerged over the ages moved (and continue to move). At the beginning of the Mesozoic Era, these lands were united in a **single enormous supercontinent**, known as Pangea, which was divided into two parts: **Gondwana** to the south and **Laurasia** to the north. Surrounding Pangea and extending across the planet was a 'superocean', known as **Panthalassa**.

WHY IS IT IMPORTANT TO UNDERSTAND HOW THE CONTINENTS MOVED?

So we can understand, for example, why we find the bones of a certain dinosaur both in America and in Asia. The animals did not swim across the oceans: they simply travelled on land **from one place to another** before the lands separated!

THE GEOLOGIC ERAS

4000 million

600 million

Scientists have identified the different geologic eras that make up the timescale of the planet's formation. Each era is in turn divided into periods. The five eras are: Precambrian, Palaeozoic, Mesozoic, Cainozoic and Neozoic.

PRECAMBRIAN
4000–600 million years ago

The Precambrian Era is **the oldest on Earth's timescale**. At this time, Earth undergoes many changes: important **Ice Ages** followed by periods of intense **volcanic activity**.

The Precambrian Era is essential, because **life develops** during this time! Our planet begins to populate itself with small organisms which, little by little, transform into more complex creatures.

PALAEOZOIC
600–250 million years ago

In the Palaeozoic Era, **the majority of creatures evolve:** Precambrian microorganisms transform into crustaceans and molluscs, and the first species of reptiles, fish and amphibians appear.

The first **mountain ranges** rise, **forests** grow, and the emerged lands, which were previously divided into two large masses, unite and form **Pangea**.

million

65 million

2.5 million

Today...

CAINOZOIC
65–2.5 million years ago

MESOZOIC
250–65 million years ago

NEOZOIC
2.5 million years ago–TODAY

The Mesozoic is known as the 'era of reptiles', because Earth is dominated by **dinosaurs**! These enormous reptiles colonize the skies, oceans and emerged lands, which once again **fragment**.

The name 'Mesozoic' derives from the Greek mésos, 'in between', a perfect name for an era located between the Palaeozoic and Cainozoic.

About 65 million years ago the Cainozoic Era began. Dinosaurs are now extinct and **mammals** and many other species disseminate, whose descendants populate the planet today.

During the Cainozoic Era **primates** evolve, that is, the first apes, from which we humans descend!

Some consider this time to be the last period of the Cainozoic, that is, the Quaternary. Others believe it is an era in itself. **We live in the Neozoic Era**, when **humans** make their first appearance and different **animal species** develop, some still present today, like us humans.

This era is still very young, so it is not easy to know when it will end, but some scientists believe there will be a new Ice Age...a long, long time from now!

MESOZOIC

The Mesozoic Era, which lasted about 185 million years, is divided into three main periods: Triassic, Jurassic and Cretaceous. During this time, temperatures were much higher and the climate rainier than today, which is why life and forests developed, with green plants and shrubs.

TRIASSIC
251–201 million years ago

JURASSIC
201–145 million years ago

CRETACEOUS
145–66 million years ago

What is the earth like in the Triassic period?

Towards the end of this period, Pangea begins to **fragment** into smaller continents: the emerged lands 'slide' on the planet's soft layer, the asthenosphere. When the lands collide, **mountains** form.

How does the earth change?

Pangea separates and allows the formation of the **central Atlantic Ocean**. The tectonic movement of the plates intensifies, leading to the birth of **mountains** and the increase in **volcanic activity**.

What happens to the emerged lands?

There are **two major continents**: Laurasia in the north and Gondwana in the south. Some segments of these two masses, however, are already starting to break away: North America is separating from Eurasia, South America from Africa, from which Antarctica, Australia and India are, in turn, separating.

Why is it important?

Dinosaurs appear in the Late Triassic period. For the most part, they are small, fast and agile, fundamental traits for surviving in a very hot and dry climate, where prey is scarce.

What other living things are there?

Small mammals, turtles as long as one metre (3.28 feet) and prehistoric crocodiles appear, as **pterosaurs**, large flying reptiles, cut through the skies. There are forests of ferns with areas of conifers and cycads, similar to the palm tree.

What plants grow?

The ecosystem is dominated by **gymnosperms** and conifers. Imagine, almost all conifers present today have their origin here at the end of this period, and we can still see a gymnosperm dating back to that time: the **ginkgo**, which was very widespread during the Jurassic period.

What creatures populate the earth?

The **oceans teem with life**, with coral reefs, deep-water invertebrates and large predators (both reptiles and squid-like animals). Dinosaurs live on land, and the skies are filled not only with pterosaurs but also with the **first species of birds**.

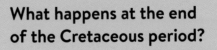

What is the climate in the Cretaceous period?

The climate is **warmer** and more **humid** than it is today, perhaps because volcanic eruptions are very frequent, as are the movements of the seabed. In the polar regions, it is not yet cold. In fact, these regions are covered not in ice but in lush forests.

What happens at the end of the Cretaceous period?

The Cretaceous ends quite tragically: with the largest **mass extinction** in history, exterminating many marine invertebrates, dinosaurs and marine and flying reptiles.

THE DINOSAURS

Scientists have so far identified more than 1,000 different species of dinosaur, which they classify according to the dinosaur's traits. This type of classification is called taxonomy.

WHAT ARE DINOSAURS?

Dinosaurs are **reptiles**, now extinct, very often gigantic in size, other times not larger than a cat. They lived during the Mesozoic Era and disappeared at the end of the Cretaceous period. Some were big and slow, others small and fast. Some preferred a solitary life, and others, instead, lived in groups. They could be **carnivores**, **herbivores** or **saprophagous** (feeding on carrion). Some walked on all fours, while others were bipedal.

WHEN DO DINOSAURS APPEAR?

The first dinosaurs, which were small carnivorous reptiles, appeared about **245 million years ago**, around the beginning of the Middle Triassic. Over time, these reptiles developed and reached truly incredible dimensions, dominating the earth for approximately 180 million years.

WHAT DOES 'DINOSAUR' MEAN?

The word dinosaur comes from Greek and means 'terrible lizard': it is composed of the words *deinòs*, meaning 'terrible', and sauros, which means 'lizard'.

DEINÒS + SAUROS = DINOSAUR
(terrible)   (lizard)   (terrible lizard)

WHERE DO THE NAMES OF DINOSAURS COME FROM?

Dinosaur names usually come from **Greek and Latin terms**, and usually end with *saurus*, which means 'lizard'. Let's take an example: the name **Ceratosaurus** is composed of *keratos*, which means 'horn', and *saurus*, 'lizard', and together become 'horned lizard'. Sometimes, however, dinosaurs are named after the **scholars** who discovered the new species or from the **place** where the fossils were found.

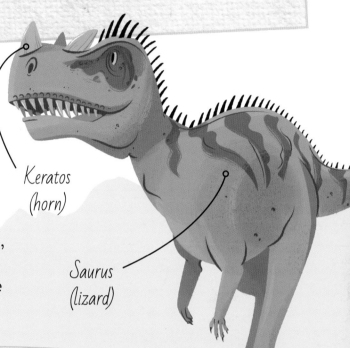

Keratos (horn)

Saurus (lizard)

WHICH IS THE FIRST-KNOWN DINOSAUR?

The first-known dinosaur is the *Eoraptor lunensis*. It was a biped, measured about one metre (3.28 feet) long and had limbs equipped with claws. It was a very **fast runner** and probably ate insects and lizards. Its skull was found in **1993** in Argentina by Paul Sereno and his collaborator Ricardo Martinez. Sereno claimed that it was the **most prehistoric**, because it did not have any of the typical characteristics of dinosaurs dating to subsequent times. The discovery allowed Sereno to confirm the theory that all dinosaurs descended from **small carnivorous bipeds**.

ANATOMY

SAURISCHIAN DINOSAURS

Saurischian dinosaurs had a **pelvis** similar to that of the reptile, which we still see in reptiles today...for example, the **crocodile**. Among the members of this order are the Tyrannosaurus, Brontosaurus and Diplodocus. The two main groups of saurischian dinosaurs are **theropods** and **sauropods**. The first dinosaurs were all saurischian. The first ornithischian dinosaurs did not appear until the Late Triassic period, about 225 million years ago.

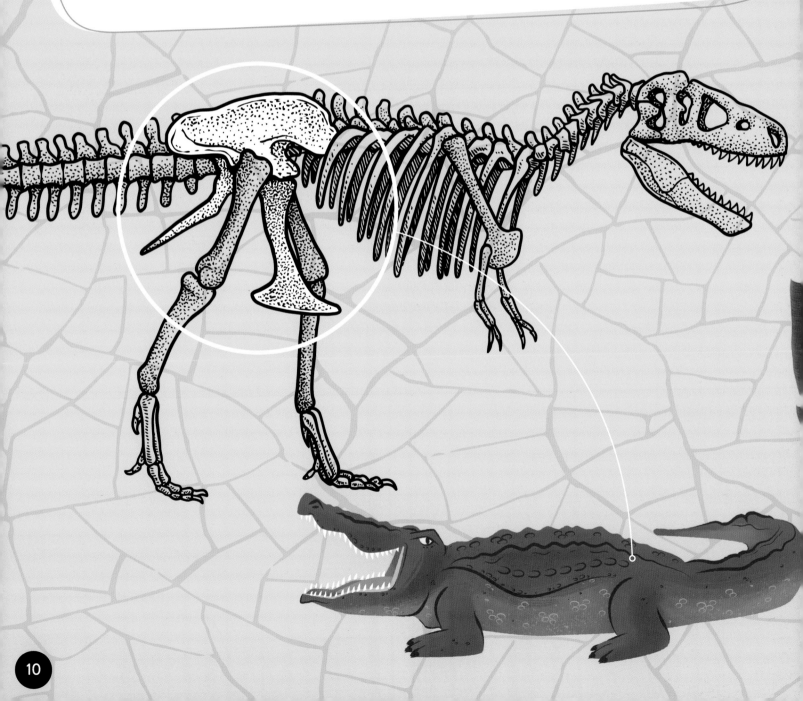

WHAT IS THE DIFFERENCE BETWEEN THEROPODS AND SAUROPODS?

Theropods are gigantic dinosaurs that walked on their **hind limbs** and had **short**, **clawed forelimbs**. They also possessed a long **tail** that was **very strong**, a subcategory which included the majority of **carnivorous** dinosaurs, such as the Tyrannosaurus.

  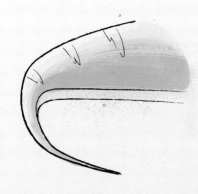

Sauropods, on the other hand, are **herbivores** and this suborder includes the largest animals that have ever lived on Earth since the Jurassic. These lived in marshes and estuaries. They had **long necks** and **small heads**, massive bodies and limbs with large claws, and **walked on all fours**.

ORNITHISCHIAN DINOSAURS

Dinosaurs that had a **pelvis similar to that of a bird** are called 'ornithischians'. This name, in fact, derives from the Greek word ornis which means 'bird'. In the upper area of the mouth they had a **'dental bone'**, very much like a beak. This category includes various species with very different characteristics. Both the Stegosaurus and the Iguanodon, for example, are ornithischians.

WHAT IS THE DIFFERENCE BETWEEN CERAPODS AND THYREOPHORANS?

Cerapods are **herbivorous** dinosaurs. They are divided into: **ornithopods**, which moved on two or four legs and had a highly developed chewing apparatus; **pachycephalosaurs**, which were bipedal and had very thick forehead bones; and **ceratops**, characterized by horns and bony growths at the back of the skull.

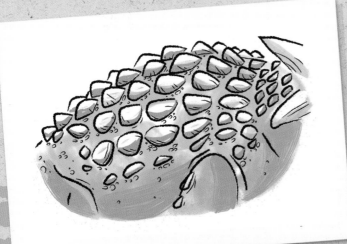

Thyreophorans, on the other hand, include the families of the Stegosaurus and the Ankylosaurus. Their main feature is the **bony protective plates** that on the Stegosaurus were located only along the spine, while on the Ankylosaurus, covered the whole body. They had flat skulls, **leaf-shaped teeth**, beak-shaped mouths, and walked on all fours.

DINOSAUR RECORDS!

27 metres (89 feet)

THE LONGEST
Diplodocus

1 metre (3.28 feet)

THE SMALLEST
Compsognathus

CARNIVOROUS DINOSAURS

Carnivorous dinosaurs ate meat. They used their swift, sharp claws as well as their cunning to catch prey. They made up about 40% of all creatures that lived in the Mesozoic.

WHAT ARE THEIR MAIN CHARACTERISTICS?

Their **bodies** were muscular but stocky: they had very strong hind **legs**, extremities similar to those of birds, and short, thin forelimbs. Their **tail** was low and strong, which served to balance the power of the hind legs. Their **jaws** were strong and powerful, able to break bones and mince flesh; some had blade-like **teeth**, others serrated or with curved tusks. Their **eyes** were small but their vision was

formidable and, thanks to a **brain** more developed than the herbivores', they could strategically organize attacks.

WERE ALL CARNIVORES ENORMOUS?

No, not all. There were smaller ones, such as the **Compsognathus**, which measured from 60 centimetres (23.62 inches) to one metre (3.28 feet) and fed on small mammals and reptiles, eggs and insects.

Carnivorous dinosaurs can be divided into three groups: carnosaurs, coelurosaurs and ceratosaurs.

CARNOSAURS

Carnosaurs lived during the Late Jurassic and Cretaceous periods. This group includes large **bipedal theropods**, which had evolved into predators of large herbivores. Most had jaws with **dagger-like teeth** curved inward, suitable for tearing flesh. The Allosaurus was a member of this category.

CERATOSAURS

Ceratosaurs shared many of the characteristics of the Allosaurus, but they were a more primitive group of theropod. The most peculiar difference compared to the carnosaurs was **a fourth claw**: dinosaurs similar to the Allosaurus had only three.

COELUROSAURS

Coelurosaurs included small and medium-sized bipedal theropods. In the 20th century the Tyrannosaurus had been classified in this group, but this theory was disproved (in part). Included in this group are all carnivorous dinosaurs closely **related to birds** and **prehistoric birds themselves**. The first examples appeared in the Late Jurassic period.

WHICH IS THE MOST FAMOUS CARNIVORE?

The **Tyrannosaurus**! It lived about 68 million years ago, during the Late Cretaceous period. It could weigh as much as 9 tons and measure over 12 metres long (39.37 feet). An unmistakable feature was its **front limbs**, short and bent at the elbow, with only two digits. The back limbs, on the other hand, were highly developed, muscular and with solid bones, needed to support and **balance the weight** of the whole body, including an impressive head and long tail which were very heavy.

WHAT DOES 'TYRANNOSAURUS' MEAN?

The scientific name, *Tyrannosaurus rex*, means 'Tyrant Lizard King'. And it's a fitting name! It was in fact the true king of the dinosaurs: **a daunting, ferocious creature**. Despite the discovery of larger dinosaur fossils, the Tyrannosaurus holds its reputation.

TÝRANNOS + SAUROS + REX = TYRANNOSAURUS REX
(tyrant)   (lizard)   (king)   (Tyrant Lizard King)

WHERE DID THE TYRANNOSAURUS LIVE?

In **forests with a warm and temperate climate**, because it was a cold-blooded animal. That is, it could not produce its own heat inside its body but absorbed it from the environment. It probably lived **near water courses**, but away from marshes and swamps, as it needed stable ground to move with agility.

WHICH FAMILY DID THE TYRANNOSAURUS BELONG TO?

The **tyrannosaurid** family, which includes different carnivorous dinosaurs that lived during the Cretaceous period. Their main features were:

- **bipedal gait,**
- **teeth as sharp as knives,**
- **large dimensions,**
- **large elongated skull.**

WHAT IS THE LARGEST TYRANNOSAURUS SKELETON EVER DISCOVERED?

Sue, named in honour of Sue Hendrickson, who brought it to light in 1990 in South Dakota (United States). From studies performed on the skeleton, 'Sue' is believed to be a **female** who died at 28 and measured more than 12 metres (39.37 feet)—and her weight was recently estimated at 9 tons!

FEARSOME PREDATORS

SPINOSAURUS

Do you think the Tyrannosaurus is the largest carnivore? You would be incorrect, because the Spinosaurus was **longer** and heavier! Its skull was elongated, like that of a crocodile. It had **conical teeth**, good for feeding on fish. It is not known precisely what the **sail** on its back was for: perhaps to regulate body temperature or to store fat.

Period: Late Cretaceous
Length: 18 metres (59 feet)
Weight: 22 tons
Distinguishing features: 'Sail' on the back

VELOCIRAPTOR

The small size of the Velociraptor made it **agile** and **fast**. It had long sharp claws to kill its prey and a tail with ossified tendon reinforcements which enabled it to **balance** on one leg while handling its prey.

Period: Late Cretaceous
Length: 1.8 metres (5.91 feet)
Weight: 45 kg
Distinguishing features: Sharp claws

DILOPHOSAURUS

The Dilophosaurus had **two bone crests** growing on its head, which made it look truly menacing! Of considerable weight and size, it was also **agile** and **fast**, and thanks to its strong hind legs, could run at great speed.

Period: Early Jurassic
Length: 6 metres (19.69 feet)
Weight: 500 kg
Distinguishing features: Double head-crests

ALLOSAURUS

Half the length of the Allosaurus's body was its **tail**. It had very powerful hind legs, but the front limbs were shorter (not as small as those belonging to the Tyrannosaurus, however!), equipped with three curved claws, to most likely grab its prey. It had short **crest-like horns** in front of its eyes. It fed on ornithischians and small sauropods, but some think it was a 'scavenger' (fed on carcasses).

Period: Late Jurassic
Length: 10.5 metres (34.45 feet)
Weight: 2 tons
Distinguishing features: Crest-like horns

OVIRAPTOR

The Oviraptor **hatched its eggs** like the birds of today do. It had strong hind legs and front limbs with three curved claws. It had a very small skull, disproportionate to its **large eyes** which were surrounded by a bony ring. It had no teeth but **powerful jaws** shaped very similar to a beak.

Period: Late Cretaceous
Length: 1.8 metres (5.9 feet)
Weight: 30 kg (66.14 lbs)
Distinguishing features: Big eyes

ALBERTOSAURUS

This dinosaur is thought to have evolved from the Tyrannosaurus! It had in fact the (presumed) **habits and characteristics of the T-rex:** well-developed hind legs, reduced forelimbs, and large, sharp, serrated teeth. It is also thought that, at least in part, the Albertosaurus fed on **carrion**, and that it frightened other predators in order to steal their prey.

Period: Late Cretaceous
Length: 9 metres (29.53 feet)
Weight: 2 tons
Distinguishing features: Serrated teeth

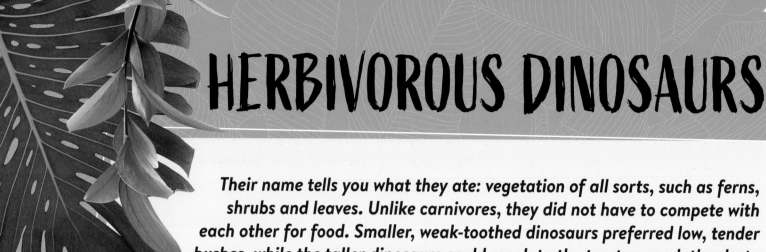

HERBIVOROUS DINOSAURS

Their name tells you what they ate: vegetation of all sorts, such as ferns, shrubs and leaves. Unlike carnivores, they did not have to compete with each other for food. Smaller, weak-toothed dinosaurs preferred low, tender bushes, while the taller dinosaurs could reach to the treetops and, thanks to their more developed teeth, shred the leaves.

WHAT ARE THE MAIN CHARACTERISTICS OF HERBIVORES?

Herbivores had physical structures that enabled them to feed on plants and ferns. Saurischian sauropods (which include the Brachiosaurus and Diplodocus) had a **very long neck** and a **large intestine** with **gastroliths** that helped to digest huge quantities of vegetation. Ornithopods (which include the Iguanodon and Triceratops) instead had special cheeks to deposit food to ruminate.

WHAT ARE GASTROLITHS?

Some sauropods used types of **stones** in their stomach to **grind**, with the help of the gastric muscles, the leaves torn by the dinosaurs' soft teeth.

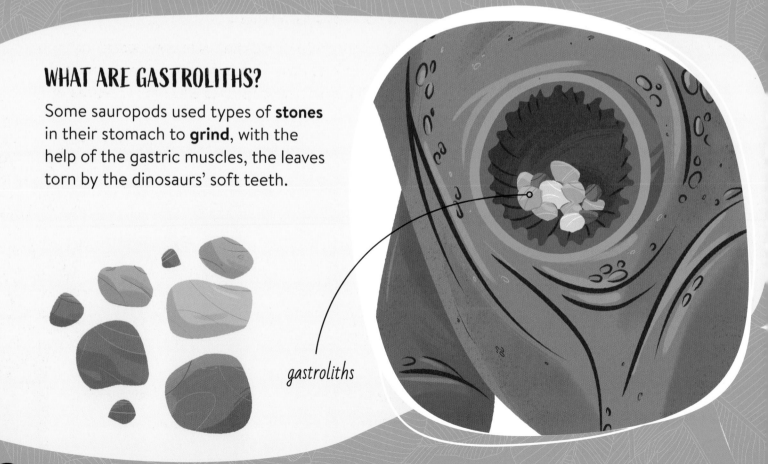

gastroliths

WHAT KINDS OF TEETH DID HERBIVORES HAVE?

Depending on the types of plants they ate, herbivores had differently shaped teeth. Those that ate more tender leaves and fruits had **leaf-shaped teeth**, useful for tearing. Those that, on the other hand, ate tougher leaves and fruits, belonging to conifers and palms, had peg-like teeth that enabled them to grind the food. Still other dinosaurs had a hard beak to tear leaves. The shape of the teeth, therefore, allows palaeontologists to deduce what dinosaurs ate.

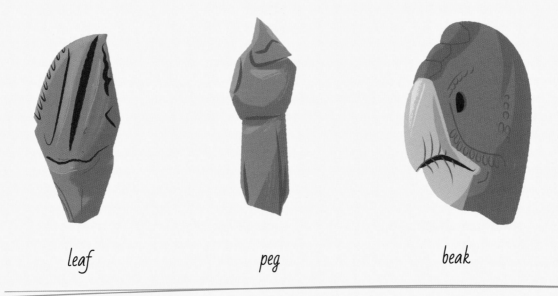

leaf   peg   beak

WERE THERE ENOUGH PLANTS FOR EVERYONE?

Herbivores were numerous, and sauropods, given their size, needed to eat a lot to make their huge bodies function at their best. To satisfy everyone's appetite, during the existence of dinosaurs, **new species** and **new varieties** of plants developed.

Horsetails
(Triassic)

Pine cones and
cycad fruits
(Jurassic)

Flowering plants
(Cretaceous)

DID HERBIVORES LIVE IN HERDS?

Many sauropods are thought to have lived in herds. We know this from the **sequences of fossil footprints** discovered. Probably these herds moved in search of food, and based on the size of the footprints discovered, it can be deduced that the adults arranged themselves in such a way as to **protect the young** from predators.

11 metres (36.09 feet)

WHICH HERBIVORE HAD THE LONGEST NECK?

The **Mamenchisaurus**! Imagine, its neck could measure as long as **11 metres (36.09 feet)!** The neck was so long that the Mamenchisaurus had a hard time bending it, but this neck was very useful for easily reaching the **tops of the tallest trees!**

HOW DID THEY DEFEND THEMSELVES?

To protect themselves from predators, dinosaurs adopted various measures: some lived in **groups**, others had **spikes**, still others **horns** or **bony plates**... some dinosaurs looked like tanks!

WHAT ARE HADROSAURS?

Hadrosaurs were **duck-billed dinosaurs**, with a large flat beak similar to a duck's. They used their hind legs for **running and walking**, while their front limbs served as a **support** when grazing. Though all of the same family, different species had **distinctive traits**: some had nasal sacs they used to communicate, others emitted bellow-like sounds and possessed hollow crests that served as sounding boxes.

Charonosaurus

Brachylophosaurus

Saurolophus

Shantungosaurus

Amurosaurus

WHICH WERE THE LARGEST HERBIVORES?

These were the **long-necked sauropods**, which to this day are still the largest, longest and heaviest land animals that ever existed. Despite the majesty of their bodies, **their heads were very small**. The front limbs were equipped with special claws which likely were used to grab branches.

LEAF DEVOURERS

BRONTOSAURUS

The Brontosaurus walked on **four stout legs**. Its long neck was balanced by an equally developed tail, which measured more than half the length of its body, most likely used as a **whip** to defend against predators. It lived on dry land, in **marsh areas**.

Period: Early Cretaceous
Length: 27 metres (88.58 feet)
Weight: 38 tons
Distinguishing features: Long neck

STEGOSAURUS

An **armoured dinosaur**, the Stegosaurus was covered in bony plates similar to shields, which served both for defence and to regulate body temperature. At the end of its tail were **four spikes**, used to scare away predators when it felt threatened.

Period: Late Jurassic
Length: 9 metres (29.53 feet)
Weight: 2 tons
Distinguishing features: Bony plates

PARASAUROLOPHUS

A **tube-like crest** about 2 metres (6.56 feet) long grew on the head of this dinosaur. Its purpose is not known precisely, perhaps to send out a call. This dinosaur had a long, **very mobile tail**, which even enabled it to swim.

Period: Cretaceous
Length: 10 metres (32.81 feet)
Weight: 2 tons
Distinguishing features: Tube-like crest

BRACHIOSAURUS

This dinosaur's head, small and flat, was characterized by **large nostrils**, believed to be used for a sharper sense of smell as well as to keep its head cool. They were covered by a **membrane** which created a sort of resonance chamber that amplified sounds.

Period: Early Cretaceous
Length: 25 metres (82.02 feet)
Weight: 80 tons
Distinguishing features: Large nostrils

TRICERATOPS

The skull of the Triceratops featured **two long horns** placed above the eyes and **one horn** positioned above the nose. It had a crest bordered by a row of bones similar to **small spears**, which formed a kind of crown. Its mouth had strong, sharp teeth and ended in a sort of **beak**.

Period: Cretaceous
Length: 9 metres (29.53 feet)
Weight: 7 tons
Distinguishing features: Three horns

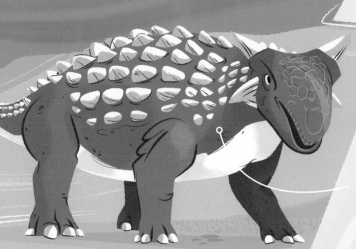

ANCHYLOSAURUS

This dinosaur's body was covered with **bony plates**, which protected it from attacks from predators. **Bony points** also protruded from the sides of its body. Even its head was armoured! Its tail ended in a kind of **'club'**, which it swung to chase away predators.

Period: Late Cretaceous
Length: 10 metres (32.81 feet)
Weight: 4 tons
Distinguishing features: Armoured head

PTEROSAURS

Pterosaurs were the rulers of the prehistoric skies.
They weren't dinosaurs or even birds: they were flying reptiles of different sizes and characteristics.

WHAT DOES 'PTEROSAUR' MEAN?

The term 'pterosaur' derives from Greek. It is composed of the words *pteron*, which means 'wing', and *sauros*, which means 'lizard'. Therefore ptero saur means 'wing lizard'.

PTERON + SAUROS = PTEROSAUR
(wing) (lizard)   (wing lizard)

WERE THEY CARNIVORES OR HERBIVORES?

For the most part, pterosaurs were carnivores. Those that lived near water hunted **fish**, **crustaceans** and **squid**, and those that flew over land ate **carcasses**, **insects**, **eggs**, small prey and **baby dinosaurs**.

WHAT WERE THE BONES OF PTEROSAURS LIKE?

The bones were **hollow** and **full of air**. This allowed them to be extremely **light**. We find this same trait in the **birds of today!**

DID THEY HAVE FEATHERS?

Not exactly. Some species had a sort of **plumage**, while others, as recently discovered, were covered in a **fur** made up of hair-like filaments, **pycnofibres**, which perhaps served to regulate body temperature. By studying certain fossils, the remains of melanosomes were found, that is, cellular structures for the **colouring of feathers**. Therefore, the feathers of these flying reptiles were most likely coloured!

HOW DID THEY REPRODUCE?

Scholars believe that pterosaurs were **oviparous**: they laid eggs. They also think that they behaved like crocodiles and turtles: they **buried** these eggs until they hatched.

WHAT WAS THEIR HEAD LIKE?

Their head was supported by a **long neck** which allowed the head to turn in all directions. The **skull** was often **elongated** and equipped with needle-shaped teeth.

The **crest** was an identifying trait, of various shapes: some consisted of bone, others a membrane like a sail, and others, soft tissue.

Under the beak, there was at times a **pouch**, which closely resembled that of the pelican.

WHAT WAS THE PURPOSE OF THE CREST?

The answer is not known for certain. However, there are **various hypotheses:**

*to regulate
body temperature*

*to direct flight
like a type of rudder*

*to choose
a mate*

WHAT WERE PTEROSAURS' WINGS LIKE?

These were not really wings, more like **membranes** formed of **skin** and **muscle**, similar to a bat's wings. These membranes stretched from four long digits to the hind limbs, but some species also had wings between shoulders and wrists and between the hind limbs.

HOW DID THEY MOVE?

For the most part they moved only by **flying**. Some possessed a truly majestic wingspan and could fly at incredible speeds...even **108 km/h (67 mph)!** There were some, however, that also managed to **walk** on their hind legs.

...AND FLYING CREATURES

Pterosaurs were not the only flying creatures of the Mesozoic. There were also other flying creatures, which can be considered the true ancestors of birds.

WHAT IS THE ARCHAEOPTERYX?

The Archaeopteryx is considered **the oldest bird**. Its name, in fact, derives from Greek and means 'ancient feather' (or 'wing'). It lived during the Jurassic period, about 150 million years ago.

WHY IS IT CONSIDERED A PREHISTORIC BIRD?

Because its **bone structure** closely resembles that of **today's birds**. The Archaeopteryx could not fly, however, because its pectoral muscles were underdeveloped, so in order to move it made **hovering jumps** from one tree to another. Further, it is thought that it scratched the ground, similar to what chickens do. Also in common with these birds, its eyes were supported by a **bony ring** surrounding them.

WHY IS THE FIRST FOSSIL OF THE ARCHAEOPTERYX SO IMPORTANT?

Because it represents a fundamental piece in our knowledge of evolution. It is the **link between dinosaurs and birds**, possessing characteristics common to both reptiles (clawed fingers and teeth) and birds (pins and feathers).

DID ALL PREHISTORIC BIRDS FLY?

No, not all. The **Hesperornis**, for example, a prehistoric bird in every way, did not have wings suitable for flight, but rather used them like oars to **move around in water**.

Hesperornis

WHAT BIRDS TODAY ARE LIKE THE HESPERORNIS?

Penguins! The **penguin** shares similar traits in both appearance and habits: it lives in aquatic environments, its body perfectly adapted to this type of life. And like the penguin, the Hesperornis was very graceful in water, but quite clumsy on land.

33

RULERS OF THE SKY

PTERODACTYL

The Pterodactyl is the **first pterosaur known to science**. Its teeth help us determine the specimens' age. Adults had about 90 teeth and the youngest, 15. This allows us to understand how the **diet might have changed with age**: perhaps the young ate only insects, while adults also consumed small animals, molluscs and fish.

Period: Between the Late Jurassic and the Late Cretaceous
Wingspan: 1 metre (3.28 feet)
Distinguishing features: A very long digit

Period: Early Jurassic
Wingspan: 1.7 metres (5.58 feet)
Distinguishing features: Quadruped

DIMORPHODON

This pterosaur was quite **clumsy**. It had short wings and a heavy skeleton, which kept it from flying long distances. So, its **flight** was **fast and short**, like a chicken's! Its skull was somewhat bulky, similar to a toucan's.

QUETZALCOATLUS

This pterosaur is **the largest flying reptile** of all time: similar in size to a giraffe! Its name derives from the Aztec language and means 'feathered snake'. It is believed that it caught its prey in low vegetation in order to conserve energy for its enormous body to function. It had a toothless beak that never closed completely.

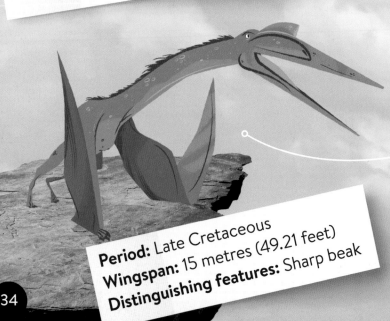

Period: Late Cretaceous
Wingspan: 15 metres (49.21 feet)
Distinguishing features: Sharp beak

TAPEJARA

This pterosaur's name means 'to be ancient'. Some scholars think that its beak and crest had **bright colours**. The crest, moreover, probably had a shape similar to an axe. It is not certain what it ate: some scholars believe it ate fruit, others fish, and still others carcasses.

PTERANODON

The Pteranodon had **powerful pectoral muscles** to move its expansive wings and travel long distances. It had a toothless beak, so did not chew its prey (mainly fish) but swallowed it whole. From these two features it derives its name, which means **'winged and toothless'**.

Period: Cretaceous
Wingspan: 7 metres (22.97 feet)
Distinguishing features: Toothless beak

PTERODAUSTRO

This pterosaur's beak was particular. Elongated and **curved upwards**, it could reach 30 centimetres (11.81 inches) long. Its lower jaw had thousands of **flexible bristle-like teeth**, perhaps for filtering water and feeding on plankton, crustaceans and algae. It had powerful legs and **broad feet**, testifying to the fact that it spent much time on the ground.

Period: Early Cretaceous
Wingspan: 2 metres (6.56 feet)
Distinguishing features: Nocturnal reptile

AQUATIC CREATURES

WHAT IS A PLESIOSAUR?

Plesiosaurs were **marine reptiles** with a very long, flexible neck. They fed on small aquatic creatures, mainly fish. It is believed that to hunt they **moved their head** from side to side in schools of fish and that they captured their prey with their long, sharp teeth. To travel in the water, they moved their fins similar to the way **sea lions** do. When they swam, it was as if they were flying through the waves.

WHICH IS THE LARGEST SPECIES OF PLESIOSAURS?

The **Elasmosaurus**. It had a **very long neck**, which could reach 7 metres (22.97 feet) in length, composed of more than 70 vertebrae! It hunted its prey underwater, suddenly appearing from below to capture it with its powerful jaw and **sharp teeth**. It travelled by moving its four fins up and down simultaneously. It possessed no gills so had to **rise to the surface** to breathe.

Earth's water expanses in this period were populated by truly different fauna: from sea turtles to crocodiles, from Plesiosaurs to Pliosaurs, as well as many other marine reptiles. None of them, however, was considered a dinosaur.

HOW IS A PLIOSAUR DIFFERENT FROM A PLESIOSAUR?

Pliosaurs had **shorter necks**, **larger heads** and **powerful jaws and teeth** to attack large prey. They also had four large fins to swim in the Mesozoic seas. The Pliosaur belongs to the order Plesiosauria, which in Greek means 'near to the lizard', which also includes the Plesiosaurs.

WHAT IF THE LOCH NESS MONSTER WERE A PLESIOSAUR?

Surely you will have heard of the **sea monster** sighted in Scotland's Loch Ness. According to these sightings, the creature has a very long neck, which led some to believe it may be a **Plesiosaur that escaped extinction!**

WHAT IS THE 'FISH LIZARD'?

Its scientific name is **Ichthyosaur**. It measured about 2 metres (6.56 feet) and had a body similar to that of a **porpoise**. Its jaws were long and equipped with sharp teeth. It had **enormous eyes**, which scientists think were used to distinguish large shapes even from far way, such as the shapes of Pliosaurs, which preyed on it. Palaeontologists believe it could reach speeds of up to **40 kilometres (24.85 miles) per hour!**

DID MARINE LIZARDS REALLY EXIST?

Yes, **Mososaurs** lived in the Cretaceous period. They had bodies similar to snakes with a backbone of more than **100 vertebrae!** They had an **elongated snout**, similar to that of the family of lizards known as the Varanidae. They also had a **particular mouth**: the bones of the upper jaw were joined by ligaments that allowed them to lower their mandible and broaden their bite to feed on large prey. The **Platecarpus** was the most widespread species of this family.

WERE THERE TURTLES IN THE MESOZOIC ERA?

Yes! There were sea turtles, such as the **Archelon**, a giant sea turtle that lived in the Late Cretaceous. They had a carapace similar to that of today s sea turtles, but much larger, reaching **3.5 metres (11.48 feet)** in length, roughly the size of a car.

WHICH REPTILES LIVED BOTH IN WATER AND ON LAND?

Notosaurs could live both in water and on land, so their limbs were not as specialized for swimming as those of the Pliosaurs or Plesiosaurs. Therefore, Notosaurs used not only their limbs but also their whole body, in an **undulating movement**, to travel through the water.

WHAT ARE THE PLACODONTIA?

They are an order of aquatic reptiles which resembled **seals** and lived in the Triassic period. Compared to other marine reptiles, they were rather 'small', barely reaching **2 metres (6.56 feet)** long. In some cases their bodies were **armoured**, similar to turtles, such as the Placochelide. It is believed they fed on shellfish.

WHAT WAS THE MOST WIDESPREAD GROUP OF MARINE CREATURES?

Molluscs, in particular ammonites, bivalves and gastropods. For example, **Orthoceratids** lived until the Late Triassic: huge molluscs with a special thick cone-shaped shell, measuring up to 2 metres (6.56 feet) in length. There were also the **Rudists**, large bivalves in the shape of an inverted cone or horn.

Ammonites

Orthoceratids

Rudists

NOT ONLY DINOSAURS

During the Mesozoic Era, the land was populated by more than dinosaurs. Insects, amphibians, prehistoric mammals, as well as plant species of all different kinds shared the earth with the enormous reptiles.

WHAT KIND OF INSECTS EXISTED IN THE MESOZOIC?

In the Jurassic period, in particular, insects were the **most abundant terrestrial invertebrates**. There were Odonates (like dragonflies), Beetles (like scarabs), Diptera (like flies) and Hymenoptera (like bees, ants and wasps).

WHY IS IT IMPORTANT TO KNOW THAT BEES LIVED IN THE JURASSIC?

Because bees, today, feed on flowering plants (**angiosperms**): this fact allows us to hypothesize that, probably, in the Jurassic period this type of plant was already present, or that bees used **other strategies** to survive.

WERE THERE MAMMALS?

Yes, they were animals that descended from the **synapsid reptiles** that survived the extinction at the end of the Permian period (the final stage of the Palaeozoic Era). During the Mesozoic Era these animals were quite **small**, similar in appearance and size to today's shrews, and were mostly **omnivores**.

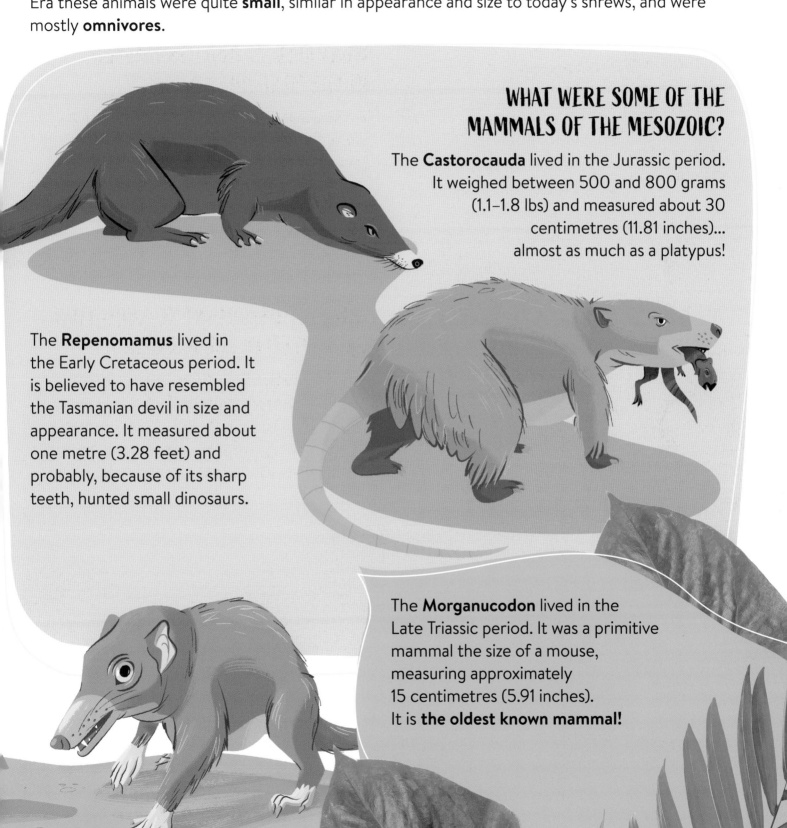

WHAT WERE SOME OF THE MAMMALS OF THE MESOZOIC?

The **Castorocauda** lived in the Jurassic period. It weighed between 500 and 800 grams (1.1–1.8 lbs) and measured about 30 centimetres (11.81 inches)... almost as much as a platypus!

The **Repenomamus** lived in the Early Cretaceous period. It is believed to have resembled the Tasmanian devil in size and appearance. It measured about one metre (3.28 feet) and probably, because of its sharp teeth, hunted small dinosaurs.

The **Morganucodon** lived in the Late Triassic period. It was a primitive mammal the size of a mouse, measuring approximately 15 centimetres (5.91 inches). It is **the oldest known mammal!**

THE EXTINCTION OF THE DINOSAURS

WHY DO DINOSAURS NO LONGER EXIST?

After roaming the earth for 150 million years, the dinosaurs disappeared in a very short time, victims of **one of the largest mass extinctions on our planet**: a **catastrophic event** which **caused more than half of all living species to disappear.** Was it a volcanic eruption? Or the impact of a giant asteroid? This great mystery of palaeontology has been solved only in the last few years!

WHAT HAPPENED?

Our planet is continually hit by **meteorites**, small rocks that disintegrate as they enter the atmosphere. Occasionally some reach the earth's surface, and a hypothesis has been put forth: if a large enough celestial body had hit the earth, the impact would have been similar to an explosion, dispersing an **extraordinary amount of dust** that would **block sunlight** for long enough to cause many species to disappear.

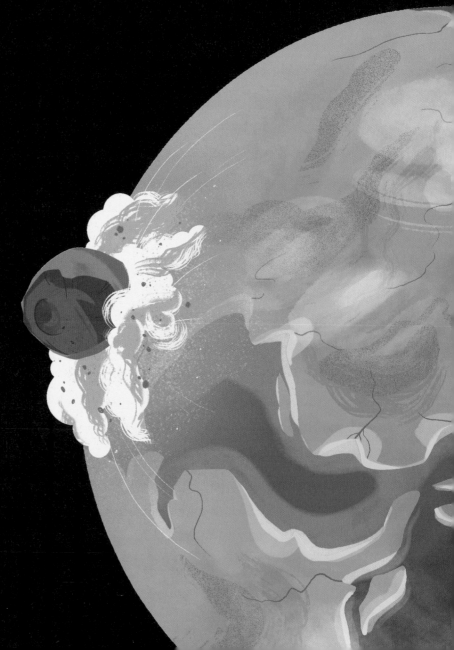

IS THIS POSSIBLE TO PROVE?

Yes, by looking for **iridium**, which is very rare on the earth's surface but **very abundant in meteorites**. If an asteroid hit Earth 66 million years ago, iridium would be abundant in the layer of rock that corresponds to the time the dinosaurs disappeared.

HOW IS IRIDIUM MEASURED?

Physicists discovered that by launching particles, **neutrons**, at certain substances, including iridium, these particles become **radioactive**, in turn emitting other particles that can be measured with different instruments. Therefore, to discover how much iridium is present in a rock, we can irradiate it with neutrons, that is, launch neutrons at it, to **measure its radioactivity** and learn how much iridium is present.

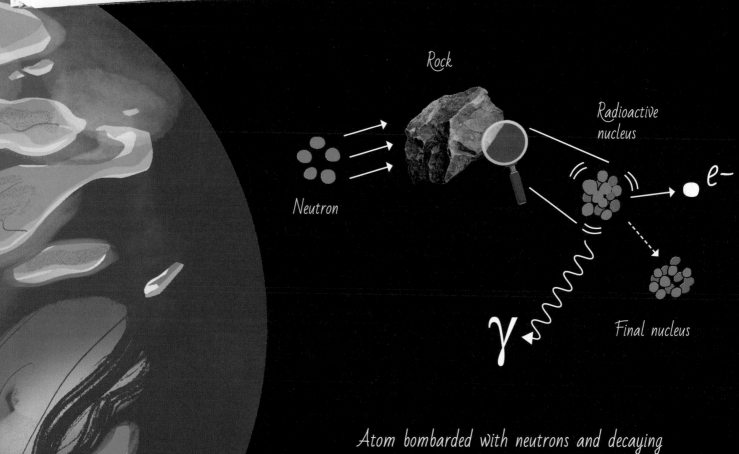

Atom bombarded with neutrons and decaying

WHAT SAMPLES HAVE SCIENTISTS STUDIED?

Scientists have studied **samples** from various places in Europe (Denmark, Italy) and elsewhere (Pacific Ocean, Caribbean Sea). In Italy one of the most famous sites is the **Bottaccione Gorge** (near Gubbio). In the samples, collected from such distant places, they found in the layer of rock corresponding to the period in which the dinosaurs disappeared a **much higher quantity of iridium** (about 20 times more) than in the earlier and subsequent rock layers.

Gulf of Mexico

WHAT OTHER CLUES DO WE HAVE?

Additional evidence that extinction may have been caused by an asteroid are the tektites found in the layers of rock dating to this period: **tektites** are a kind of **glassy rock** present in areas where meteorite showers have occured.

Tektites

Mexico

WHEN WAS THE IMPACT SITE DISCOVERED?

Towards the end of the 20th century, the impact site was identified. A celestial body—probably an asteroid between 10 and 80 kilometres (6.21 to 49.71 miles) in diameter—struck the **Yucatan Peninsula** in **Mexico** with a massive destructive impact.

Chicxulub crater

100,000 billion tons

WHAT WERE THE CONSEQUENCES OF THE IMPACT?

This immense shock, estimated to be greater than a **100 trillion-ton explosion**, jettisoned enormous amounts of dust into the atmosphere, **obscuring the Sun** for a long time. Immediately after the collision, a **huge tsunami** swept through what is now the Gulf of Mexico. Evidence of this catastrophe, in the form of sediments carried by the tsunami, have been found as far away as Cuba.

ARE THERE ANY OTHER HYPOTHESES ABOUT THE EXTINCTION OF THE DINOSAURS?

Some scientists believed such a collision was insufficient to cause extinction. They argued, in fact, that **massive volcanic eruptions** could release dust into the atmosphere and with large quantities of carbon dioxide and other toxic gases, and perhaps even a certain amount of **iridium**.

DID ONLY THE DINOSAURS GO EXTINCT?

No. With the dinosaurs **more than half the animal world disappeared**, including pterosaurs and large marine reptiles. Some groups of animals, however, managed to **survive**: birds, small terrestrial reptiles, mammals, turtles and crocodiles have descended to us from that time.

HOW DO WE KNOW FOR CERTAIN IT WAS AN ASTEROID?

To be certain it was the great impact of an asteroid that caused the extinction, the event would have had to happen **before the dinosaurs' disappearance**. About ten years ago a group of scientists improved rock dating techniques and determined that the two events occurred **'simultaneously'**: that is, both within a 30,000-year interval.

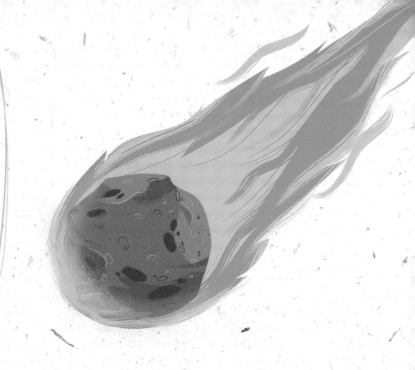

HAVE WE REACHED A DEFINITIVE ANSWER TO THIS MYSTERY?

Palaeontologist **Pincelli Hull** with her research group managed to solve this enigma. Based on earlier evidence and using what we know today about the functioning of our planet's ecosystem, she analysed the data on **marine fossils** collected in the last 40 years and confirmed that **the impact of a gigantic asteroid** was enough to cause the disappearance of the dinosaurs and many other living species. This research was published in 2020.

AFTER THE DINOSAURS

At the end of the Cretaceous period, a new era began, the Cainozoic, from about 66 million years ago to today. This era is divided into three periods: Paleogene, Neogene and Quaternary or Neozoic, although, recently, the era has been divided into the Tertiary and Quaternary. Life in the Cainozoic was very different from life in the Mesozoic.

CAINOZOIC

66 million years ago		23 million years ago		2.6 million years ago		Today
PALEOGENE		**NEOGENE**		**QUATERNARY**		
Palaeocene	Eocene	Oligocene	Miocene	Pliocene	Pleistocene	Holocene

56 million years ago   33.9 million years ago

5.3 million years ago

11,700 years ago

WHAT CHANGES OCCUR IN THE FLORA?

Already from the end of the Cretaceous we witness a great diffusion of **angiosperms**, that is, flowering plants. During the Cainozoic the **climate begins to differentiate**: deciduous angiosperms, for example, begin to develop mainly in the colder regions, while evergreen varieties become mainly localized to the subtropics and tropics.

WHAT HAPPENED WITH THE COLLISION OF THE CONTINENTAL PLATES?

The collision of the tectonic plates gave birth to **the largest mountain ranges** in the world. The Alps and the Carpathians in southern Europe, the Atlas range in north-western Africa and the Himalayas in Asia were caused by the collision of the African plate and Indian plate which moved towards the Eurasian plate. At this time also, the Rocky Mountains rose in North America as well as the Andes Cordillera in South America.

WERE THERE SIGNIFICANT EVENTS DURING THIS ERA?

During the Cainozoic, a **great extinction of mammals** occurred between 10,000 and 8,000 years ago. It is believed there were two major causes: **climate change** following the melting of the Pleistocene glaciers and excessive hunting by the Palaeolithic humans. **Hunting** by humans is considered the most likely reason, because hunting tools had become increasingly advanced.

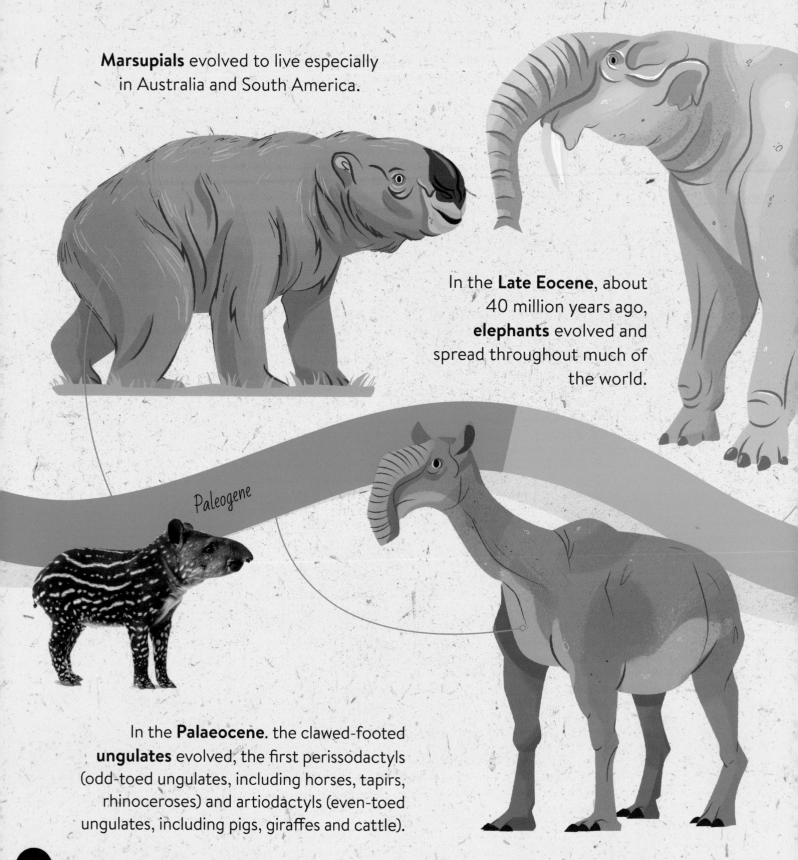

Marsupials evolved to live especially in Australia and South America.

In the **Late Eocene**, about 40 million years ago, **elephants** evolved and spread throughout much of the world.

Paleogene

In the **Palaeocene**. the clawed-footed **ungulates** evolved, the first perissodactyls (odd-toed ungulates, including horses, tapirs, rhinoceroses) and artiodactyls (even-toed ungulates, including pigs, giraffes and cattle).

During the Cainozoic there was a rapid diversification of life forms, and the mammals, in particular, evolved.

The **first modern humans** appeared in the **Pleistocene**.

Quaternary

Neogene

In the **Pliocene**, forests and plains were populated by **gigantic mammals**, such as the **sabre-toothed tiger**, **giant sloths** and **mammoths**. In this period the first hominids appeared.

DINOSAUR FOSSILS

The information we have about the different types of dinosaurs has come down to us through the fossil remains. Palaeontologists use this information to understand how and where these prehistoric creatures lived, what they ate, how they reproduced and which plants grew at the time. The rock, therefore, contains a photograph of the world of the past.

WHAT IS PALAEONTOLOGY?

Palaeontology is a branch of science that studies the **creatures of the geological past** and the **environments** in which they lived. **Palaeontologists** are the scholars who dedicate themselves to searching for and examining fossils.

DO ONLY THE BONES REMAIN?

In most cases, yes. Sometimes, however, it could happen that the bodies of prehistoric animals were buried in volcanic ash or sand. This would 'mummify' them, leaving clues, even about the make-up of their **skin**. Palaeontologists have also found **footprints** and **excrement**, as well as different types of **egg fossils**.

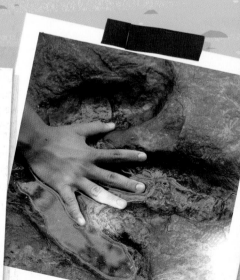

HOW DID DINOSAUR FOSSILS FORM?

Optimal conditions were necessary. The dinosaur had to be **large** enough, because the bones of smaller dinosaurs were more delicate and broke apart more easily, or were eaten by animals that ate carrion. The **spot** where the dinosaur died had to be '**suitable**', for example near a lake, so the mud would cover it making it more likely to be conserved.

1 The body of a dead dinosaur lies at the **bottom of a lake**. The flesh begins to decompose, or is eaten by fish, leaving the skeleton intact.

2 **Silt**, **mud** and **sand** cover the bones (in this way the water does not move them).

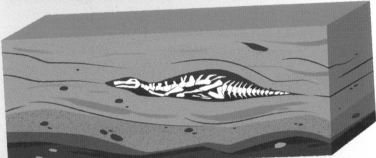

3 Over time, the bones are replaced by **harder minerals**.

4 Because of the movements of the earth's crust, the **fossilized skeleton** appears on the surface.

WHAT TOOLS ARE USED ON AN EXCAVATION SITE?

Cameras and **GPS** to document the location and position of the fossil.

Explosives or **bulldozers**, useful for crumbling the thickest layers of rock.

Tissue paper, plaster bandages, rubber moulds and **insulating materials** to safely transport fossils to the laboratory.

Numbered plates to organize the individual bone fragments found.

4

Hammers, **shovels** and **chisels** to free the fossil from the matrix. **Brooms** and **brushes** with soft bristles, to clean the soil from the fossils without damaging them.

WHAT INSTRUMENTS ARE USED IN THE LABORATORY?

Very **delicate brushes**, sometimes soaked in water or mild detergent, to remove the remains of dust or scoria from the bone.

Pneumatic air pen to clean fossils more deeply.

Corrosive substances to remove the most difficult matrix layers.

Glue to seal and reinforce the finds, to prevent them from fragmenting.

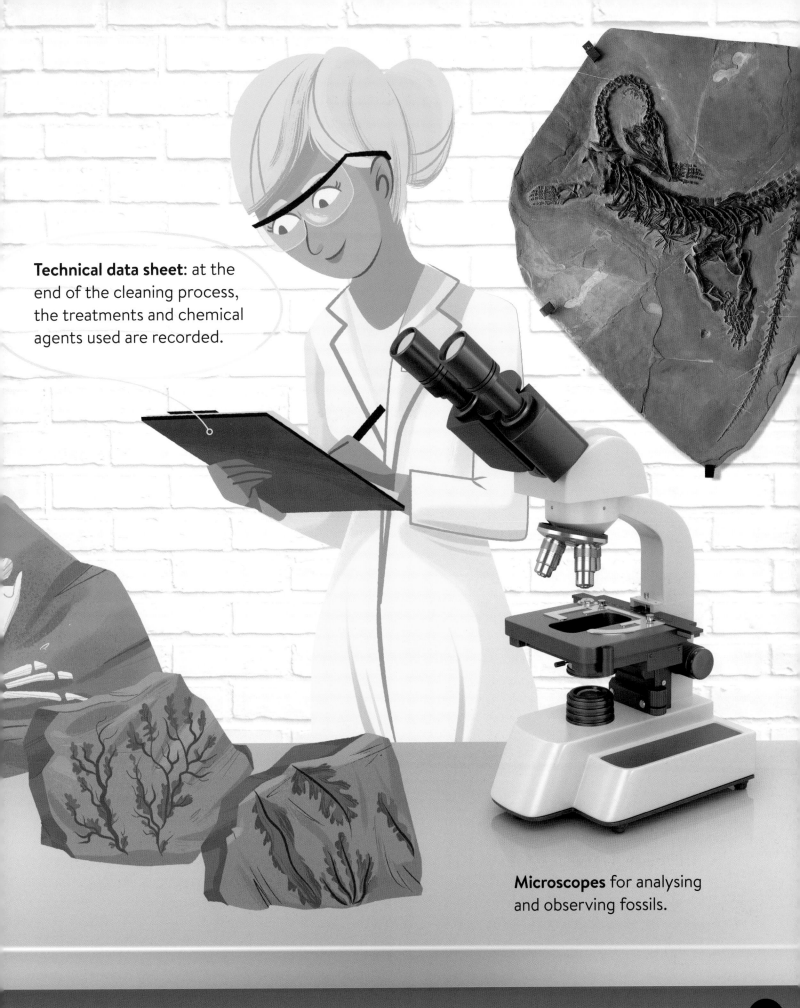

Technical data sheet: at the end of the cleaning process, the treatments and chemical agents used are recorded.

Microscopes for analysing and observing fossils.

TO THE MUSEUM

ARE COMPLETE DINOSAUR SKELETONS EVER FOUND?

Unfortunately, it happens very **rarely**. In fact, most of the time palaeontologists find only a few **isolated bones**. From there begins a complex operation to **reconstruct** the entire dinosaur. In this way we can admire these giant skeletons in museums all over the world!

WHAT ARE THE STEPS OF RECONSTRUCTION?

1 Each fossil is **carefully examined** by microscope and cleaned with special tools in the laboratories.

2 The different fossils or fragments are **assembled**. It is rare to find a complete skeleton, and because of this, palaeontologists help each other by comparing the **material in their possession** with other previously reconstructed fossils. If some bones are missing or too damaged, they are rebuilt using **fiberglass**.

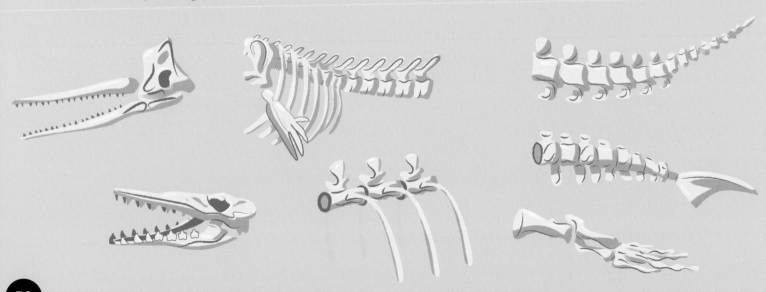

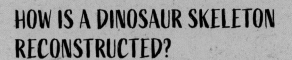

HOW IS A DINOSAUR SKELETON RECONSTRUCTED?

After finding the different components of the skeleton during excavations, the work that follows requires **care and patience.** It is essential to reconstruct the original appearance of the dinosaur, providing information on how it ate and moved.

3 Often, especially for larger dinosaurs, the whole **skeleton is recreated** using **fibreglass.** Fossils, in fact, are very heavy and delicate, and it would be too risky to exhibit them in museums! Scholars make sure to position the bones in **the most natural posture** possible.

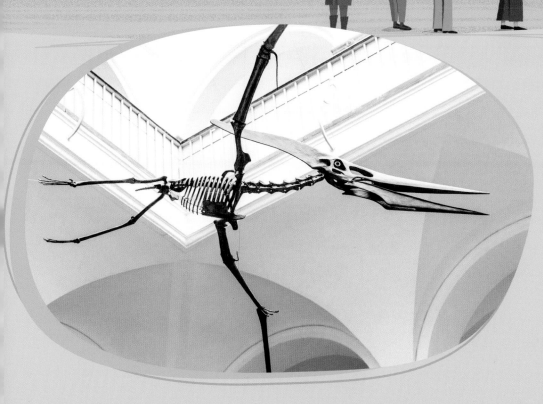

4 To support the skeletons, special **steel armour** is built, often hidden inside the bones. To support pterosaur skeletons, **wires** are often attached to the ceiling.

CREATE YOUR OWN FOSSIL

Do this activity with an adult present!

You will need:

| plasticine | a fairly deep container | water | gypsum powder | a shell | oil |

1 Work the plasticine so that it becomes soft, and place it on the bottom of the container to form a fairly thick layer.

2 Take the shell and rub the surface with oil (so it does not stick to the plasticine), and press it into the plasticine layer.

3 When the shell is well inserted, gently remove it from the plasticine layer: you will see the shell's imprint in the plasticine.

4 Mix the water and the gypsum powder and let the mixture rest for a few minutes. Then pour it in the imprint in the plasticine layer.

5 Let it dry for a few days. Once the gypsum has solidified, peel it away from the plasticine layer and you will find your shell fossil!

IDENTIFY THE REPTILE

In this book you met several reptiles: herbivorous and carnivorous dinosaurs, pterosaurs and plesiosaurs. Each of them possesses distinctive traits. Can you tell which reptile is which by reading the clues and observing the details? Write its name next to the image. (All the answers can be found in this book!)

Dilophosaurus – Parasaurolophus – Ankylosaurus – Spinosaurus
Pterodaustro – Quetzalcoatlus – Ichthyosaurus

I am bigger than a Tyrannosaurus and have straight, conical teeth that I use to feed on fish.

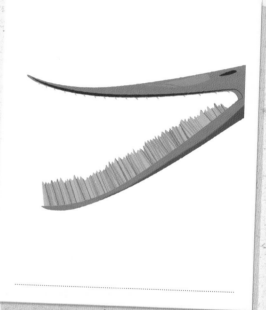

I am a nocturnal reptile and feed on algae, plankton and crustaceans.

My tail is very mobile and allows me to swim.

They also call me a 'fish lizard', and I have enormous eyes which allow me to see from far away.

I am an armoured dinosaur and my tail ends in a kind of 'club'.

I weigh a lot, but despite that I can run agilely and at great speed.

I am the largest flying reptile and my name means 'feathered snake'.

FIND THE TOOLS!

As we have read, palaeontologists use different tools to unearth fossils. Can you find some of these tools drawn below?
(All the answers can be found in this book!)